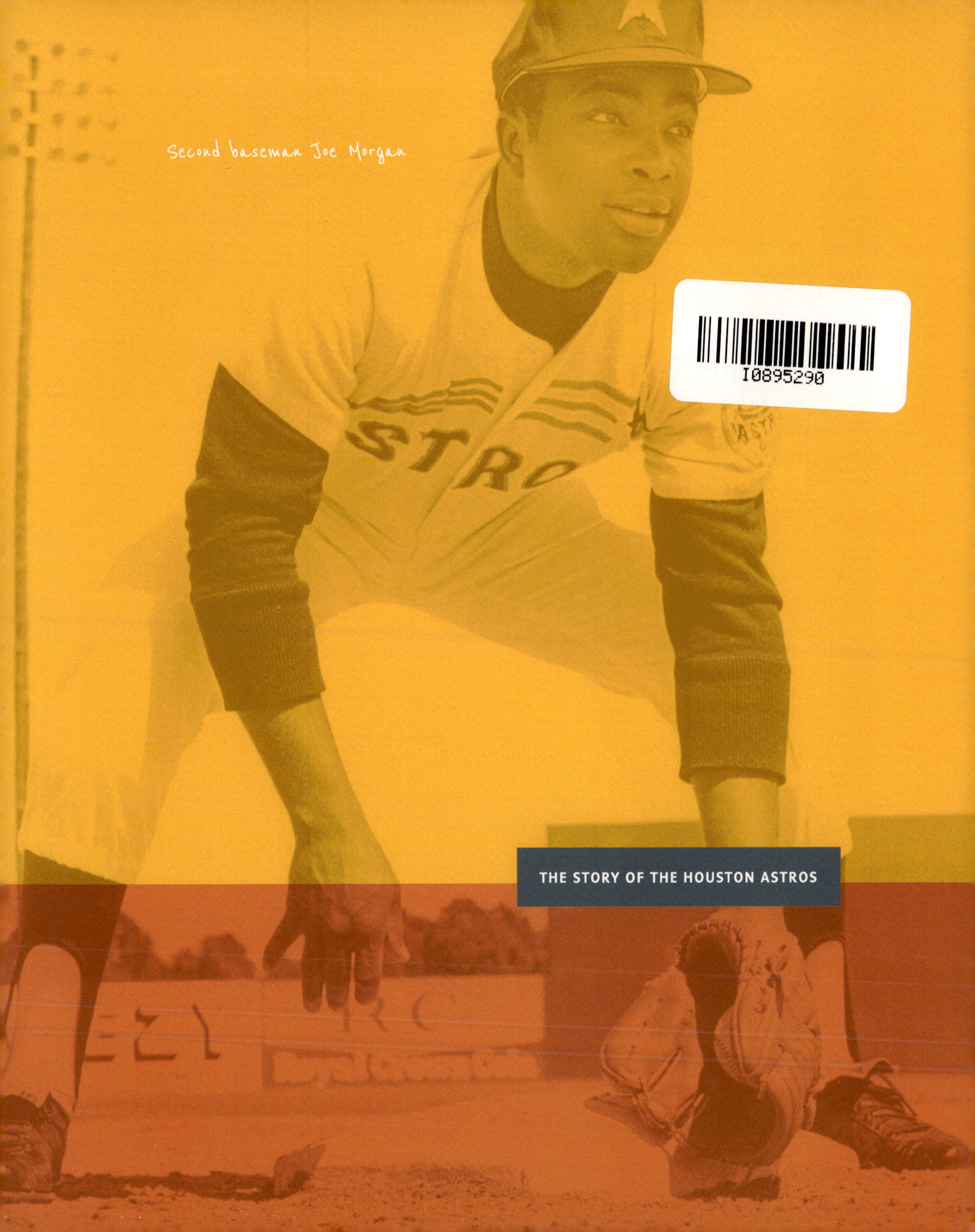

Second baseman Joe Morgan

THE STORY OF THE HOUSTON ASTROS

Second baseman José Altuve

THE STORY OF THE

HOUSTON ASTROS

JIM WHITING

Outfielder Jim Wynn

CREATIVE EDUCATION / CREATIVE PAPERBACKS

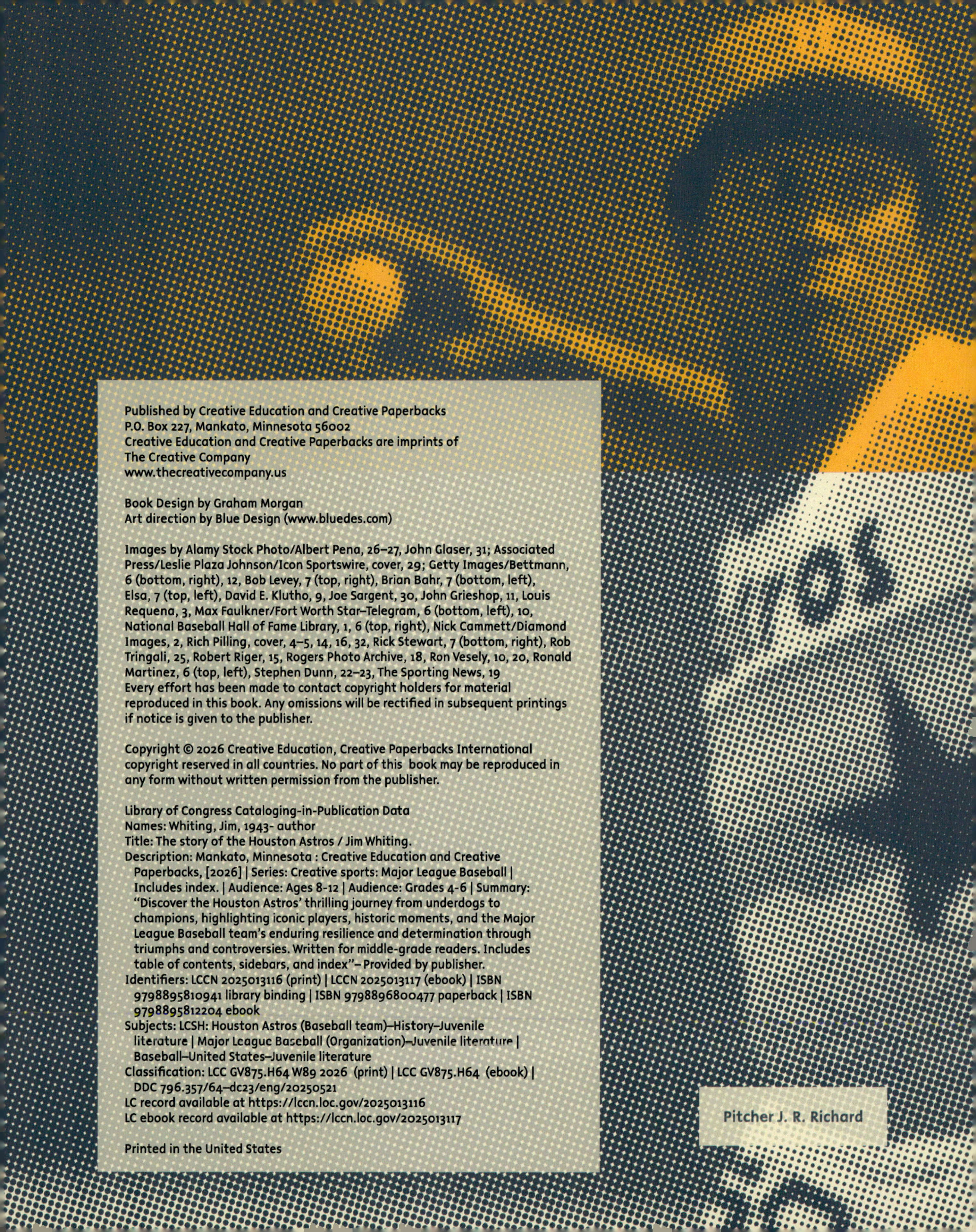

Published by Creative Education and Creative Paperbacks
P.O. Box 227, Mankato, Minnesota 56002
Creative Education and Creative Paperbacks are imprints of
The Creative Company
www.thecreativecompany.us

Book Design by Graham Morgan
Art direction by Blue Design (www.bluedes.com)

Images by Alamy Stock Photo/Albert Pena, 26–27, John Glaser, 31; Associated Press/Leslie Plaza Johnson/Icon Sportswire, cover, 29; Getty Images/Bettmann, 6 (bottom, right), 12, Bob Levey, 7 (top, right), Brian Bahr, 7 (bottom, left), Elsa, 7 (top, left), David E. Klutho, 9, Joe Sargent, 30, John Grieshop, 11, Louis Requena, 3, Max Faulkner/Fort Worth Star–Telegram, 6 (bottom, left), 10, National Baseball Hall of Fame Library, 1, 6 (top, right), Nick Cammett/Diamond Images, 2, Rich Pilling, cover, 4–5, 14, 16, 32, Rick Stewart, 7 (bottom, right), Rob Tringali, 25, Robert Riger, 15, Rogers Photo Archive, 18, Ron Vesely, 10, 20, Ronald Martinez, 6 (top, left), Stephen Dunn, 22–23, The Sporting News, 19
Every effort has been made to contact copyright holders for material reproduced in this book. Any omissions will be rectified in subsequent printings if notice is given to the publisher.

Library of Congress Cataloging-in-Publication Data
Names: Whiting, Jim, 1943- author
Title: The story of the Houston Astros / Jim Whiting.
Description: Mankato, Minnesota : Creative Education and Creative Paperbacks, [2026] | Series: Creative sports: Major League Baseball | Includes index. | Audience: Ages 8-12 | Audience: Grades 4-6 | Summary: "Discover the Houston Astros' thrilling journey from underdogs to champions, highlighting iconic players, historic moments, and the Major League Baseball team's enduring resilience and determination through triumphs and controversies. Written for middle-grade readers. Includes table of contents, sidebars, and index"– Provided by publisher.
Identifiers: LCCN 2025013116 (print) | LCCN 2025013117 (ebook) | ISBN 9798895810941 library binding | ISBN 9798896800477 paperback | ISBN 9798895812204 ebook
Subjects: LCSH: Houston Astros (Baseball team)–History–Juvenile literature | Major League Baseball (Organization)–Juvenile literature | Baseball–United States–Juvenile literature
Classification: LCC GV875.H64 W89 2026 (print) | LCC GV875.H64 (ebook) | DDC 796.357/64–dc23/eng/20250521
LC record available at https://lccn.loc.gov/2025013116
LC ebook record available at https://lccn.loc.gov/2025013117

Printed in the United States

Pitcher J. R. Richard

GIPSON
31
Houston

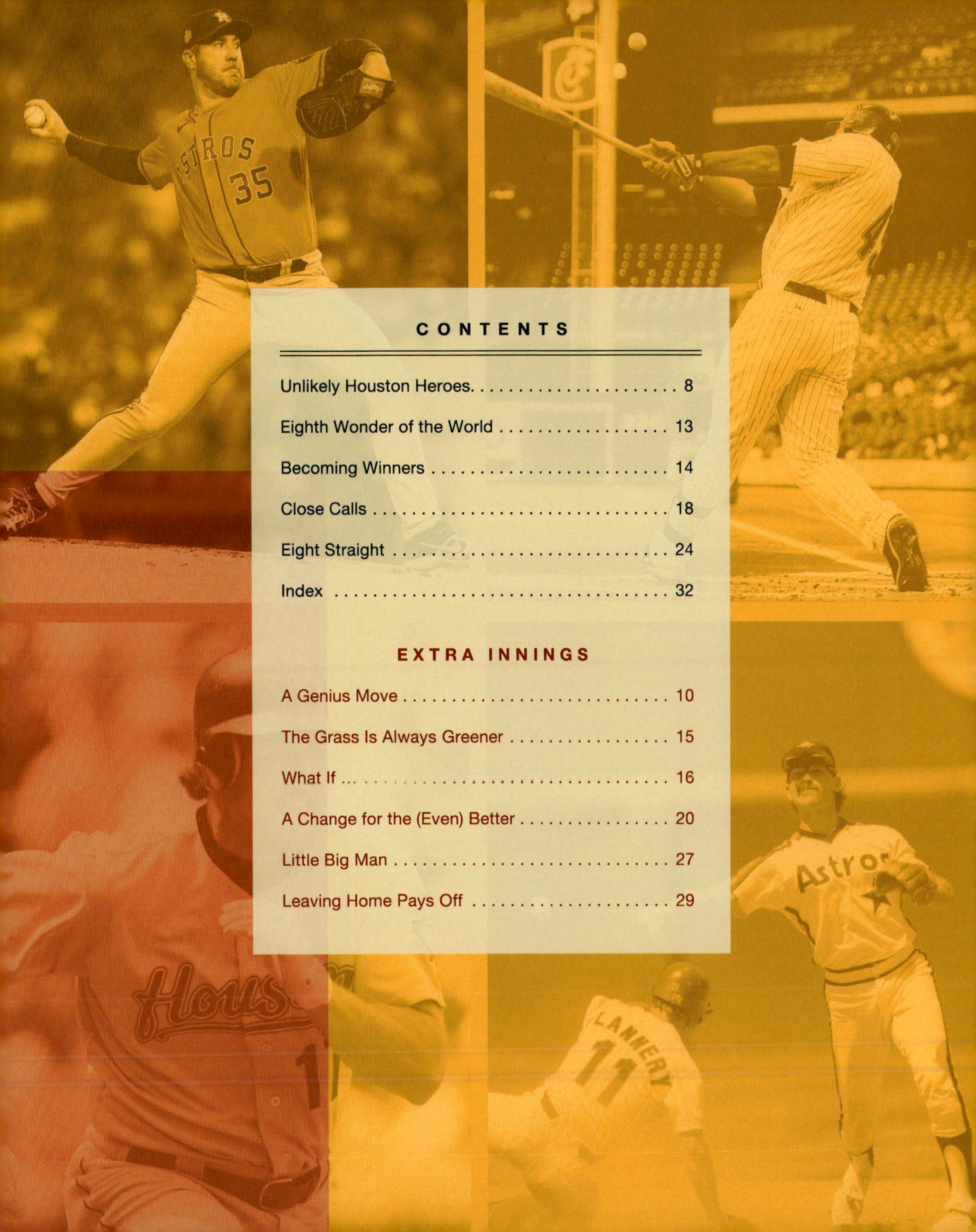

CONTENTS

Unlikely Houston Heroes 8

Eighth Wonder of the World 13

Becoming Winners 14

Close Calls 18

Eight Straight 24

Index 32

EXTRA INNINGS

A Genius Move 10

The Grass Is Always Greener 15

What If 16

A Change for the (Even) Better 20

Little Big Man 27

Leaving Home Pays Off 29

UNLIKELY HOUSTON HEROES

The Houston Astros began playing Major League Baseball (MLB) in 1962. But as the years went by, fans were disappointed that the team never played in the World Series. At the start of the 2005 season, it looked like the disappointment would continue. A seven-game losing streak that began in mid-May dropped the team's record to 15–30 (.333 winning percentage).

Then the team caught fire. From that point, they compiled a 74–43 (.632) mark for an overall 89–73 record. Now they faced the Atlanta Braves in the best-of-five National League Division Series (NLDS). The Astros won two of the first three games. But they still needed one more win to advance to the National League Championship Series (NLCS). The winner of the NLCS would play in the World Series.

In the top of the third inning of Game 4, Houston starting pitcher Brandon Backe walked two Atlanta batters and hit a third to load the bases. Atlanta's Adam LaRoche made Backe pay for the miscues with a grand slam home run. In the bottom of the eighth, Houston trailed 6–1. Then Astros outfielder Lance Berkman blasted a grand slam to narrow the score to 6–5. But the first two Houston hitters in the bottom of the ninth inning made outs. That

Outfielder/first baseman Lance Berkman

LANCE BERKMAN
OUTFIELDER/FIRST BASEMAN
ASTROS SEASONS: 1999–2010
HEIGHT: 6-FOOT-1
WEIGHT: 220 POUNDS
KEY STATS: .296 BATTING AVERAGE, 326 HOME RUNS, 1,090 RBIS, 5X ALL-STAR

EXTRA INNINGS

A GENIUS MOVE

Lance Berkman's dad played college baseball. From an early age, he taught his son how to hit. "Ever since I could walk, I've had a bat in my hand," Berkman said. It paid off. Berkman had an outstanding college career as a first baseman. He led the NCAA in 1996 with 41 homers and 134 runs batted in (RBIs). The Astros made him their first-round pick in 1997 (16th overall) because of his bat. There was one problem. The Astros already had a first baseman, future Hall of Famer Jeff Bagwell. To get his bat into the lineup, Houston made him an outfielder. It was a genius move. Berkman ranks in the top 10 in Houston history in many offensive categories. He is first in on-base percentage (.410) and second in home runs (326).

Catcher Brad Ausmus

brought catcher Brad Ausmus to the plate. He was one of the league's best defensive catchers but had hit only three home runs during the season. He defied the odds and hit a fly ball that barely cleared the left-center field fence. That tied the score at 6–6. The game went to extra innings.

Inning after inning, the score remained tied. With one out in the bottom of the 18th, Houston rookie utility player Chris Burke, who had entered the game as a pinch-runner in the 10th inning, came to bat. He had hit just five homers during the season. Burke slammed the ball into the left field stands. He rounded the bases and leaped into the mob of his teammates crowding home plate. Houston won 7–6! It was one of the greatest moments in team history.

"From a hitter's standpoint, that's one of those rare moments when you're looking to drive a ball," Burke said. "I put the right swing on it and got it up and over the wall. From there, it was all fun and games."

The 18 innings were the longest postseason game in MLB history. The ball that Burke hit and his jersey are in the Baseball Hall of Fame.

The Astros went on to win the NLCS and advance to the World Series for the first time. If not for those long balls by two unlikely heroes—Ausmus and Burke—they might never have made it.

EIGHTH WONDER OF THE WORLD

In 1961, the American League (AL) expanded from 8 to 10 teams. The National League (NL) did the same thing in 1962. One of the new NL teams was in Houston. The franchise was named the Colt .45s. It was a nod to the famous pistol of the Old West. The Colt .45s misfired in their first three seasons. They did not win more than 66 games each time.

The team's home field, Colt Stadium, presented its own problems. Mosquitoes attacked fans in the open-air seating. Day games were scorching. Night games were not much cooler. Rattlesnakes occasionally slithered across the outfield grass. Harris County Domed Stadium resolved those issues. It opened in April 1965. Houston became the first team in MLB to play under a dome.

Co-owner Roy Hofheinz called the stadium the "eighth wonder of the world." The ceiling rose 208 feet above the field at its highest point. An internal weather station helped keep the temperature comfortable. Fans enjoyed cushioned seats.

Before the first game, Hofheinz changed the team's name to the Astros. It referred to America's space program, which was headquartered in Houston. At the same time, the new facility became known as the Astrodome. Unfortunately, the team continued losing.

In 1969, the league split into two divisions. Houston played in the NL West Division. The Astros reached .500 for the first time. They won 81 games and lost 81. One reason was powerhouse outfielder Jim Wynn. "The Toy Cannon" stood 5-foot-10 and weighed a mere 160 pounds. His bat had a lot of "pop," considering his small size. He connected for 33 homers.

Outfielder Jim Wynn sliding into home

Pitcher J. R. Richard

In 1972, consistent batting and pitching gave the Astros their first winning season. They went 84–69. All-Star center fielder César Cedeño was a big factor in their success. He won the first of five straight Gold Glove awards. "There must be something Cedeño can't do well," Cincinnati Reds manager Sparky Anderson said, "but I haven't found it yet."

During the rest of the 1970s, Houston focused on its pitching staff. J. R. Richard won 20 games in 1976. In 1978, he topped the majors with 303 strikeouts. Knuckleballer Joe Niekro tallied 21 wins in 1979. The team led the NL West for most of that season. But the Reds pulled ahead near the end. The Astros finished second in the division by one and a half games. Only the division winners advanced to the playoffs.

BECOMING WINNERS

The Astros acquired strikeout king Nolan Ryan before the 1980 season. He notched his 3,000th career strikeout on July 4. Niekro's knuckleball continued to baffle batters. Richard was on his way to having his best season. Then tragedy struck. On July 30, Richard suffered a stroke. He never returned to baseball. Even without him, the Astros kept winning. They topped the NL West for the first time. They earned their first trip to the

THE GRASS IS ALWAYS GREENER

The Houston Astros moved into the Astrodome in 1965. The roof was made of semitransparent panels. Those panels let in sunlight. But players found it hard to track fly balls. Team officials had the panels painted gray. That blocked sunlight. The grass died. The outfield turned into hard, rutted dirt. The Astros experimented with a new product. It was called ChemGrass. The bright green nylon fibers were similar to natural grass. ChemGrass soon became known as AstroTurf. Players had to relearn how to field grounders on the new surface. Other indoor sports facilities soon began using synthetic turf products.

EXTRA INNINGS

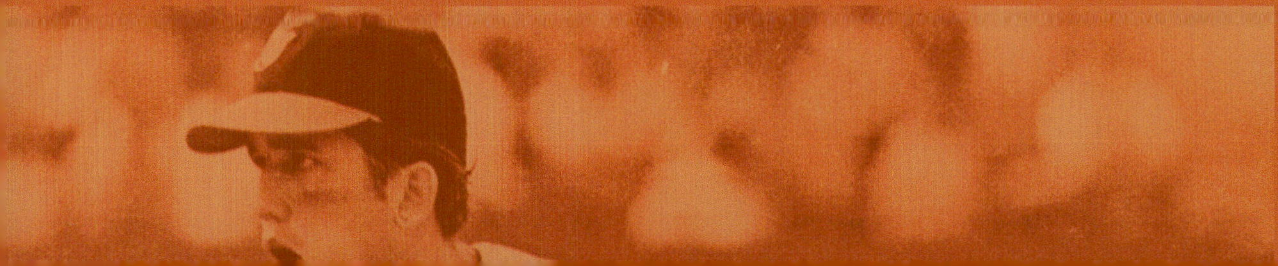

EXTRA INNINGS

Shortstop Derek Jeter

WHAT IF . . .

The Astros had the top overall pick in the 1992 MLB Draft. Former Detroit Tigers star pitcher Hal Newhouser was a scout for the Astros. He urged the team to draft shortstop Derek Jeter. The team rejected his advice. Instead, Houston picked infielder/outfielder Phil Nevin. Newhouser resigned in protest. Nevin played just 18 games with Houston. His batting average was a disappointing .117. Then he was traded. Meanwhile, Jeter was named Rookie of the Year. He went on to a stellar 20-year career with the New York Yankees. He became a 14-time All-Star with a lifetime batting average of .310. The Yankees retired his number (2) in 2017. He was voted into the Baseball Hall of Fame three years later.

playoffs. Houston faced the Philadelphia Phillies in the NLCS. Four of the five games went into extra innings. The Astros lost the series, three games to two.

In 1981, a players' strike took nearly two months out of the middle of the season. When it ended, MLB officials split the season. The first-half winners in each league played the second-half winners. Houston's 33–20 second-half record earned it a spot against the Los Angeles Dodgers in the NLDS. Once again, the Astros came up just short. Houston missed the postseason for the next four years.

Four Houston pitchers—Mike Scott, Bob Knepper, Jim Deshaies, and Ryan—each won 12 or more games in 1986. Houston won the NL West. The team played the New York Mets in the NLCS. The Mets prevailed, four games to two. Once again, the Astros had come close to their first NL pennant, only to watch it slip away.

For the next few years, Houston routinely did well until late in the season. Then, sudden slides knocked them from postseason contention. Those years also saw many roster changes. Switch-hitting rookie Ken Caminiti began manning third base in 1987. Shortstop Rafael Ramírez came on board in 1988. Houston also added catcher Craig Biggio that year. After a few years, they moved him to the field. First baseman Jeff Bagwell showed off his power hitting in 1991. He was named Rookie of the Year.

In 1994, the Astros joined the newly formed NL Central Division. They were in a tight race for the division title. But another players' strike lopped off the final seven weeks of the season. The playoffs were canceled.

Houston topped the NL Central in 1997. It faced the Atlanta Braves in the NLDS. Atlanta swept Houston in three games.

Pitcher Vern Ruhle

CLOSE CALLS

Pitcher Randy "The Big Unit" Johnson joined the team midseason in 1998. He won 10 games and lost only once. He had a microscopic 1.28 earned run average (ERA). The Astros easily took the NL Central title. They won a franchise-record 102 games. But the San Diego Padres beat them in four games in the NLDS.

Houston played its final season in the Astrodome in 1999. The team won its third straight NL Central crown. It met the Braves in the NLDS. Yet again, the Astros came up short. Fans and team officials alike hoped that playing in the new Enron Field in 2000 (later renamed Minute Maid Park) would provide a boost. But the team finished well out of playoff contention.

Pitcher Randy Johnson

CRAIG BIGGIO
CATCHER/SECOND BASEMAN
ASTROS SEASONS: 1988–2007
HEIGHT: 5-FOOT-11
WEIGHT: 185 POUNDS
KEY STATS: .281 BATTING AVERAGE, 291 HOME RUNS, 1,160 RBIS, 7X ALL-STAR

A CHANGE FOR THE (EVEN) BETTER

Craig Biggio was a catcher in high school, college, the minor leagues, and his first four years with Houston. He was an All-Star in that fourth year. But Houston manager Art Howe asked him to move to second. "He said it would extend my career," recalled Biggio. "He said it would help the team, let the team take more advantage of my speed." Biggio agreed. "I felt like a Little Leaguer again," he said of learning to play an entirely new position. The move paid off. Biggio went on to a Hall of Fame career with Houston.

EXTRA INNINGS

The Astros returned to the top of the division in 2001. Yet again, they were bested by Atlanta in the NLDS. Players and fans were frustrated. "It's a recurring theme, no question about it," Bagwell said. "We got down in a hole and never dug ourselves out." The Astros fell to second place in 2002 and 2003.

In 2004, the team's roster featured slugging outfielder Carlos Beltrán. Star pitchers Andy Pettitte and Roger Clemens ruled the mound. Houston met Atlanta again in the NLDS. Houston pounded Atlanta with 12 runs in the decisive Game 5. It was the first time the Astros won a postseason series! But they lost to the St. Louis Cardinals in the NLCS. Their long-awaited trip to the World Series was put on hold.

Houston went 89–73 the following year. The Astros again topped the Braves in the NLDS. Then they met the Cardinals for a rematch in the NLCS. Houston took the series in six games. It advanced to the World Series for the first time. The Astros met the red-hot Chicago White Sox. Chicago went on to sweep the series. Bagwell retired after the season. He played his entire career in Houston. He is the team leader in home runs with 449.

In 2006, Houston finished 82–80 and out of playoff contention. The following season was worse. The team fell to 73–89.

The Astros improved in 2008. Closer José Valverde led the league with 44 saves. The Astros held strong through most of the season. Then Hurricane Ike ravaged Texas in mid-September. The team had to play several "home games" at other fields. Their 86–75 mark missed the playoffs. Houston ended with a disappointing 74–88 record in 2009 and 76–86 in 2010. Then the bottom fell out.

Houston won just 56 games in 2011 and 55 in 2012. They moved to the American League (AL) the following season. The change of scenery didn't help. Houston tumbled to a 51–111 mark. It is the worst record in team history.

Pitcher Roger Clemens

Yet in the midst of this terrible season, *Sports Illustrated* magazine made a bold, almost unbelievable prediction. They featured the Astros on the cover of the June 24, 2013, issue. The headline read, "Your 2017 World Series Champs." Hardly anyone took it seriously. The Astros were the laughingstock of MLB. Even the hometown *Houston Chronicle* called it "more of an attention-grabbing, perhaps even tongue-in-cheek projection than a prediction." And the Astros were even worse after the issue came out. They had been 29–48 at that point. (.377 winning percentage) and tumbled to 22–63 (.259) during the rest of the season.

EIGHT STRAIGHT

Houston took a "baby step" toward realizing the *Sports Illustrated* prediction in 2014 with a 70–92 record. Their 86–76 record in 2015 was the first winning season since 2009 and first playoff appearance since 2006. They beat the Yankees in the Wild Card game but fell to the Kansas City Royals in the American League Division Series (ALDS). Houston missed the playoffs in 2016 despite a winning record.

In 2017, Houston won 101 games. Second baseman José Altuve hit .346 and was named Most Valuable Player (MVP). The Astros cruised through the ALDS against the Boston Red Sox. They beat the Yankees in the American League Championship Series (ALCS).

Then the Astros faced the Dodgers in the World Series. Houston lost Game 1, 3–1. They won Game 2, 7–6 in 11 innings, and Game 3, 5–3. After Los Angeles

Second baseman José Altuve

27
399

JOSÉ ALTUVE
SECOND BASEMAN
ASTROS SEASONS: 2011–PRESENT
HEIGHT: 5-FOOT-6
WEIGHT: 165 POUNDS
KEY STATS: .306 BATTING AVERAGE, 229 HOME RUNS, 812 RBIS, 9X ALL-STAR

EXTRA INNINGS

LITTLE BIG MAN

When he was 16, José Altuve attended an Astros tryout camp in his homeland of Venezuela. Scouts there said, "You're too short." They sent him home. Altuve's father told him to go back the next day. This time a team official asked, "Can you play?" Altuve replied, "I'll show you." He did. About a decade later, in 2017, Altuve had a season for the ages. He appeared in his fifth All-Star Game. He won his fourth Silver Slugger award. He was the AL batting champion for the third time. He helped the Astros win the World Series. The Associated Press named him Male Athlete of the Year. *Sports Illustrated* named him, along with pro football standout J.J. Watt, Sportsperson of the Year. Altuve hopes his example will open doors to those who may not look impressive at first glance. "Whoever plays well should have the right to play," he said.

evened the series in Game 4, Houston blasted five home runs to win Game 5, 13–12. The Dodgers had another 3–1 win in Game 6. Houston scored five runs in the first two innings of the decisive Game 7. They held on for a 5–1 victory. The Astros were finally world champions! The magazine cover from four years earlier had come true! Outfielder George Springer had been on that cover. Fittingly, he smashed five homers to tie the all-time record. He was named Series MVP.

The team set a new franchise record with 103 wins in 2018. It easily beat the Cleveland Indians in the ALDS. Then the Astros beat Boston in the first game of the ALCS. But the Red Sox came back to win the next four.

The Astros' 107 wins in 2019 were the most in MLB. Justin Verlander had an MLB-best 21 wins. Gerrit Cole added 20. Left fielder/designated hitter Yordan Álvarez was a unanimous selection for Rookie of the Year after batting .313 and slugging 27 home runs despite missing more than two months at the start of the season. Houston advanced to the World Series against the Washington Nationals. But Washington won, four games to three. It was the first time in World Series history that the visiting teams had won every game.

During the 2020 season, Houston was penalized for sign stealing. The team was fined $5 million and lost several draft choices. That wasn't the only issue. The Covid-19 pandemic shortened the season. Houston finished just 29–31. But MLB held an eight-team post-season tournament in each league. The Astros won the first two rounds. But the Tampa Bay Rays beat them in the NLCS.

Houston advanced to the World Series again in 2021. But it lost to the Braves, four games to two.

The Astros won 106 games in 2022. They faced the Phillies in the World Series. Philadelphia won two of the first three games. Houston bounced back to win Game 4 as four pitchers combined to throw the first World Series no-hitter in 66 years. Houston won the next two games for its second World Series title.

EXTRA INNINGS

YORDAN ÁLVAREZ
LEFT FIELD/DESIGNATED HITTER
ASTROS SEASONS: 2019–PRESENT
HEIGHT: 6-FOOT-5
WEIGHT: 237
KEY STATS: .298 BATTING AVERAGE, 164 HOME RUNS, 466 RBIS, 3X ALL-STAR

LEAVING HOME PAYS OFF

Growing up in Cuba, Yordan Álvarez dreamed of playing Major League Baseball. But he couldn't do that if he stayed in Cuba. So he defected in 2016, even though he didn't know when he would see his family again. The Los Angeles Dodgers signed him to a contract that same year. They traded him to Houston before he played any games in the United States. The Astros called him up during the 2019 season. He hit a home run in his first game. It was a sign of things to come. He has become a three-time All-Star and was named to the All-MLB first team in 2022. Houston fans have high hopes for his future with the team.

HOUSTON
3

Third baseman Alex Bregman

The Astros fell back to 90–72 in 2023. They won the ALDS over the Minnesota Twins, but they couldn't hold a 3–2 edge over the Texas Rangers in the ALCS. The Rangers clubbed 20 runs to win the last two games.

Houston got off to a slow start in 2024. At one point near midseason, they trailed the Seattle Mariners by 10 games. They rebounded to finish with an 88–73 mark and qualify for the playoffs for the eighth season in a row. That is the fourth-longest streak in MLB history and includes seven division titles. In the era of free agency in which players can sign with any team they want, that streak is especially remarkable. But they lost to the Detroit Tigers in two games in the Wild Card Series.

From their early days as the Colt .45s to their two recent World Series titles, the Astros have worked hard to live up to the larger-than-life expectations of their home state. In just over a decade, the team has gone from laughingstock to leader. Their streak of playoff appearances shows no signs of stopping. With good reason, Houston fans feel confident that their team will be among the brightest stars in the baseball galaxy for years to come.

Shortstop Jeremy Peña

INDEX

All-Stars, 10, 14, 16, 20, 26, 27, 29
All-Star Game, 27
Altuve, José, 24, 26, 27
Álvarez, Yordan, 28, 29
Astrodome, 13, 15, 18
Ausmus, Brad, 11
Backe, Brandon, 8
Bagwell, Jeff, 10, 17, 21
Beltrán, Carlos, 21
Berkman, Lance, 8, 9, 10
Biggio, Craig, 17, 20
Bregman, Alex, 31
Burke, Chris, 11
Caminiti, Ken, 17
Cedeño, César, 14
Clemens, Roger, 21, 23
Cole, Gerrit, 28
Colt Stadium, 13
division championships, 8, 14, 17, 21, 24, 31
Enron Field, 18. Also see Minute Maid Park.
Harris County Domed Stadium, 13. Also see Astrodome.
Hofheinz, Roy, 13
Howe, Art, 17, 20
no-hitter, 28
Johnson, Randy, 18, 19
Minute Maid Park, 18
MLB Draft, 16
Nevin, Phil, 16
Newhouser, Hal, 16
Niekro, Joe, 14
Pettitte, Andy, 21
playoffs
  American League Championship Series (ALCS), 24, 28, 31
  American League Division Series (ALDS), 24, 28, 31
  National League Championship Series (NLCS), 8, 11, 17, 21, 28
  National League Division Series (NLDS), 8, 17, 18, 21
  Wild Card, 24, 31
Ramírez, Rafael, 17
Richard, J. R., 14
Rookie of the Year award, 16, 17, 18, 28
Ruhle, Vern, 18
Ryan, Nolan, 14, 17
Silver Slugger award, 27
Springer, George, 28
team name, 13
Valverde, José, 21
Verlander, Justin, 28
World Series, 8, 11, 21, 24, 27, 28, 31
Wynn, Jim, 13